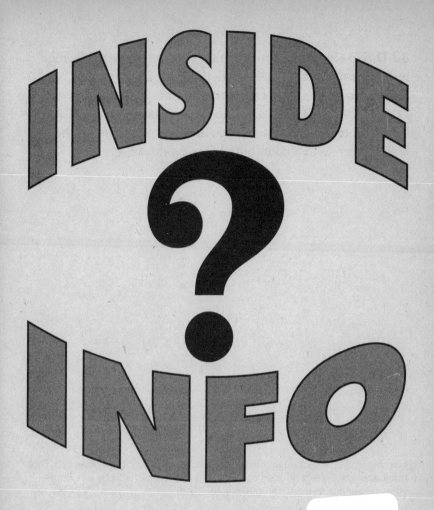

INSIDE ? INFO

JJ DeSpain

Publications International, Ltd.

JJ DeSpain writes about health, consumerism, and senior issues for national magazines in the United States and Canada. She is a former critical care nurse and has had a variety of experiences working with various government groups, including the Veterans Administration. She authored *Life-Saving Health Secrets* and coauthored *Government Secrets*.

Louis Weber, CEO
Publications International, Ltd.
7373 North Cicero Avenue
Lincolnwood, Illinois 60712

Permission is never granted for commercial purposes.

Manufactured in U.S.A.

8 7 6 5 4 3 2 1

ISBN: 0-7853-4925-1

Contents

Get the Inside Scoop!

No one tells you the whole story these days. They keep a little bit back—just enough so that things turn out to their advantage. You expect it from the government, since inside information is a way of life for Uncle Sam. But it's the same with your car dealer, funeral director, real estate agent, utility company—even your doctor. There's more to know than they're telling you.

Did the store manager step up and explain the store's price-matching policy? Of course not. He hopes you don't catch on to it, because if you do it will cost his store time and money. Did you know that you can negotiate bank fees? Bet your banker never told you that one.

And when you were doling out a week's pay to melt that cellulite away, did anyone tell you that the term "cellulite" was created as a money-making gimmick? Absolutely not. The melt-away cellulite industry is huge, and no one wants you to find out the real truth.

It's all inside information. *They* know it, *you* don't, and *they* don't want you to find out. But if a product, service, or knowledge that can make your life better is available to you, you have the right to know about it.

Deadly fumes in your home? Legionnaires' disease where you least expect it? Bogus area codes that suck $10 a minute out of your bank account?

You sure have a right to know these things—and others. Did you know that you *can* negotiate a better deal at a no-negotiation auto dealership? And that some car colors are actually safer than others? *Inside Info* will teach you these things and many, many more.

And now for the first important piece of inside information—something to get you started. Throughout this book, you'll see references to informative Web sites you should access. It's great information if you have a computer and an Internet service provider. But what if you don't? Will you miss out on something that's free and easy?

No! You can surf the waves of the World Wide Web even if you don't own a computer. Here's how:

■ Libraries have computers, and the paper for printouts is usually free. Troop on down to your library to see what's available. If you find the computer but don't know how to use it, ask a librarian.

■ Universities have them, usually in their libraries. If a school is state-funded and you're a taxpayer, walk right in and sit right down.

■ Once you've discovered the possibilities of computer technology, but want to learn more, you can do several things:

• Take a college course. (This can be expensive.)

• Take a continuing education course. (Much less expensive.)

• Look for a friend or relative who can teach you. (Pay them back with a nice lunch!)

Discovering what you're not supposed to know is great fun. You've outwitted them. You've beat them at their own game. The *Inside Info* you need to know is finally out—and victory is sweet!

I Can Do That!

Remember the little train that was faced with climbing a steep hill? He wasn't sure he could do it until he put his mind to it. "I think I can! I think I can!" You can climb that steep hill, too. With a little know-how and a can-do attitude, you'll be amazed by the things you'll accomplish.

You Ought to Be in Pictures

Look! That's you—the 113th person from the left, 62 rows back. Movie extras fill out the background, mingle with the crowd, huddle, stampede, and stand against the wall with champagne glass in hand. Here's how to get that job:

■ Register with a casting company. You don't have to live in Hollywood to do it; movies are cast in all locations. Try www. moviex.com/extras or

Call a Movie Star

Personal messages won't get through to your favorite actress. However, if you've got a great cause, call the Screen Actors Guild National Headquarters at 323-954-1600 and ask for the phone number of the *representative* of the star you'd like to contact. Since an actor's representative is the one who usually makes the scheduling decisions, this is even better than calling the star. Well, almost.

www.ep-services.com/
html/cenex.htm.

- Pay your registration fee,
  usually $10 to $20.

- You can also freelance,
  which means just show
  up at a movie set, hang
  around, and ask the assis-
  tant director for a chance
  to join the extra pack.
  Sometimes it works, sometimes it doesn't.

Cut an Album

If you can sing or play beautiful music, don't let your
talent go to waste. To start
your recording career, as-
semble a professional presentation package, including:

- A cover letter. Include one
  page saying what you want
  to do. Include your best
  professional references.

- A demo CD. Check the
  yellow pages for a recording studio that can help
  you produce your demo.

- A one-page professional
  biography. Put your best
  info in the first paragraph.

- An 8×10 black-and-white
  glossy. To have one
  snapped on the cheap, ask
  a friend to do it—or check
  out a local college for a
  photography major.

Now, find an Artist & Reper-
toire Representative (A&R
rep). This person locates and
develops talent. Try *The
Musician's Atlas* for starters.
Or contact record labels that
turn out the type of music
you perform.

FAST FACT

First ask if the A & R rep is
accepting unsolicited
submissions. If he's not,
send a catchy letter ask-
ing for permission to
submit your package.

Are You an
Origami Whiz?

Or maybe you're a master
Indian flute carver. Whatever
the case, if you have the
expertise, maybe it's time to
teach what you know to
others. Many places need

teachers, and a college degree is not required.

- Most universities have community learning or continuing education classes. Grab a current catalog to see what's being offered. If the class you'd like to teach isn't being taught, stick your resume and a class proposal in the mail.

- Contact your library. They're especially interested in classes for children.

- Call a senior citizens center. They're always in need of something new and interesting.

Turn Your Poems Into Dough

If you can write a verse to brighten someone's day,

A lucrative career may soon be on the way.

Hopefully, your poetry is a lot better than that. If it is, think greeting cards. They

make up 50 percent of all first-class mail today, which means the demand is high.

This is what you do:

- Send for writing and submission guidelines from greeting card companies. Lists and addresses can be found in *Writer's Market* or *Poet's Market* (Writers Digest Books).

- Study cards from companies to which you'd like to submit your work.

- Submit your verses as prescribed in the guidelines.

Who, What, When, Where, and Why

Ever had the secret desire to put on that cub reporter's hat and cover the story? You can do it, and it's not really as difficult as you might think. First, pick your newspaper wisely. *The New York Times* probably isn't the place to start. Instead, try local newspapers, including weeklies.

Next, think of something that's not being covered already, something that will catch the interest of the paper's readers:

- a movie or book review
- a special-interest section, such as on your hobby
- town events and organizations

Contact the editor and ask her to give you a try. Offer two or three ideas and a sample of your work, or ask about her needs for the paper. Since these papers pay little or nothing, your chances of snagging the first job are pretty good. After that, you're on your own.

On the Airwaves

You may not get the morning drive-time radio slot, but your voice could go out to thousands who are unable to read the printed word for themselves. Radio Reading programs exist in most states, and they need your voice to read:

- magazines
- newspapers
- novels

The good thing is, no experience is necessary. You can read in the studio live or record for a later airing. Many stations will even let you broadcast from your home phone in the cozy comfort of your favorite recliner.

Call your local National Public Radio or television station to see if there's a radio reading station that's near you.

Casino Capers

Don't wear that big "Duh" on your forehead when you enter a casino. Most casinos have "duh detectors" who will spot inexperienced gamblers. Even if you don't have any casino savvy, follow these tips so that you'll look like you do:

■ Never belt down too much of the complimentary booze. Casinos want to get you plastered so that you'll get faster and looser with your bets.

■ Avoid staying up as late as the casinos are open. Casinos love drowsy betters.

■ Even though they use such terms as "nickel" and "quarter," it's really $5 and $25 to you. Don't get caught up in their nickel and dime terminology. It's meant to devalue, psychologically, the amount you're betting. When this happens, you're likely to bet more.

How to Read a Poker Face

It could help your game if you know how to read an opponent. And, it can bolster your opponent's game if he knows how to read you. Bluffers usually:

■ breathe shallowly when their turn comes

■ stare at their hands

■ reach for chips out of turn

■ bet with authority

■ fling chips nonchalantly into the pot

Players with a good hand often:

■ share their hand with a bystander

■ engage in light conversation

■ lean forward in their seats, tap toes, or drum fingers waiting for their turn

■ bet with noticeable indifference

Reading the Slots

The only way you'll win against the machine is to observe its pay cycle.

■ Watch before you play. If someone dumps a boat-

Spotting the Loaded Dice

There are two ways.

1. Fill a tall glass with water and then drop the die in. Repeat this several times, turning different numbers up. If the die turns so that the same number or two keep showing, it's loaded.

2. Hold the die diagonally on opposite corners. Grip it loosely between your thumb and forefinger. If it's loaded, it will pivot when the weighted sides are on top.

load of money into a machine and gets no return, step right up when she vacates. The machine could be ending its down cycle and getting ready to pay off.

■ Offer a change clerk 10 percent of your winnings for pointing you to the hottest machine on the floor.

■ Look at the coin holders next to each machine. Several may mean they haven't been used to cart off winnings, indicating that a pay cycle could be coming. Fewer holders suggest that someone has gone to the bank to cash in recently.

Dot Gov

The government has gone online, which means you can take care of business in minutes—instead of hours, days, or weeks. Here are a few of Uncle Cyber–Sam's greatest hits:

■ At www.ssa.gov, you can:

• Request a Social Security statement of yearly earnings reported to your Social Security records. You'll also receive estimates of your entitled benefits as they would

Wanna Call the Prez?

It's a snap. You won't ring through to the Oval Office, but you can leave a message telling Mr. President exactly how you feel about anything. Call the White House at 202-456-1414 or e-mail president@whitehouse.gov or vice.president@whitehouse.gov. While you're at it, you might as well let your congressional representatives know how you feel at lcweb.loc.gov/global/legislative/congress.html.

come to you now and in the future.

- Request a replacement Medicare card.
- Ask for Form 1099—a benefits statement for the previous year.
- Request a benefit verification letter if another benefits agency requires it.

■ If you're a former federal employee, you may have some pension money coming. Check it out at search.pbgc.gov/srch-name.cfm (this one does not start with www).

FAST FACT

Many scam businesses offer to provide these free government services at a modest cost. Stay away!

Geezer.com Alert!

Don't get alarmed. Geezer originally meant merrymaker or masquerader, and in this case it means a big opportunity to sell your arts and crafts online. You don't even need a computer to take advantage of the e-commerce opportunities awaiting you. Other cyber-geezers will do it for you.

Here are the requirements:

■ You must be age 55 or over.

■ All products for sale must be handcrafted—and new.

There's a one-time, modest registration fee to sell as many items online as you wish, for as long as you like.

If you're interested, go to www.geezer.com to take a look at the products offered for sale. Then contact Green Thumb, Inc., the national nonprofit organization sponsoring Geezer.com., at www.greenthumb.org. If you're not online, call 703-522-7272 or write to Green Thumb, Inc., at 2000 N. 14th St., Suite 800, Arlington, VA 22201.

A Really Great Secret That Pays

Do you like to shop, or just browse? Maybe hoofing through the mall is high on your exercise list. If it is, you can romp into a few of the stores, look around, and earn some extra bucks as a secret shopper.

Who employs secret shoppers?

- grocery stores
- retail stores
- bars and lounges
- hotels
- restaurants
- movie theaters
- beauty salons
- insurance companies
- banks and credit unions
- Uncle Sam

And what does a secret shopper do?

- evaluates services
- fills out a report given to him by the company for which he's working

And there are often some perks besides the pay:

- free movies
- free meals
- free haircuts

To learn all the details about becoming a secret shopper, grab a copy of *Get Paid to Shop* (Business Resources Publications, 1998) at the library.

Home Sweet Home

Do you know all the secrets lurking in, and just outside, your own home? Don't worry. We're prepared to teach you Home Secrets 101, where you'll learn what you didn't know you needed to know. Learning these tips may even save your life.

Things That Go Boom in Your Mailbox

No, letter and package bombs aren't all that common, but every year 500 unsuspecting victims find them in their mailboxes. To protect yourself, look for these things:

- too much weight for the size of the package

- too much postage

- package looks lopsided or uneven

- mailed from a foreign country via airmail or special delivery

- no return address

- excessive tape or string used to secure it

- misspelled or incorrect words on the label

- stains or discoloration on the package

- protruding wires or tin foil

If you're suspicious, call your local FBI office, police department, or fire department.

And Things That Go Boom on Your Toilet Seat

E. coli can spring out of your toilet when you flush. It can explode all over the seat and everything else within several feet of the seat, including your:

  toothbrush

  soap

  washcloth and towel

  hairbrush and comb

  flush handle

The result of this bacterial contaminant is often bloody diarrhea. E. coli can even be fatal. Other bugs can also swirl up with your toilet spray, causing infectious diarrhea, intestinal woes, or hepatitis. Best defense:

  Stand up and step back when you flush.

  Better yet, close the lid before flushing.

  Keep objects with which you come in contact away from your toilet.

  Clean and disinfect your toilet several times a week.

Poisonous Plants

Thousands of plant poisonings are reported to poison centers each year. If you have any plants in and around your house, here are some poisonous culprits of which you should be aware:

■ Garden flowers: bleeding heart, daffodils, delphinium, foxglove, hens & chickens, lantana, lily of the valley, lupine, and sweet pea.

■ Houseplants: caladium, dieffenbachia, and philodendron (this can be fatal to cats).

■ Shrubs: azalea, mountain laurel, oleander, privet, rhododendron, and yew.

Virtually all reported plant poisonings happen to children. So if Junior decides to make a houseplant salad, call your local poison control center—no matter which houseplants, flowers, or shrubs he ingests.

For more information, or to find the poison control center closest to you, visit the American Association of Poison Control Centers at www.aapcc.org. If the child collapses or quits breathing, call 911.

The Cold Facts

Air conditioners cool the air in the summer, but they're expensive to run. To keep your house temperature comfortable in the most cost-effective way:

- Use awnings, drapes, and blinds to eliminate direct heat from the sun.
- Turn off the lights. They create heat.
- Use the AC sparingly and assist the cool breeze with ceiling or other ventilation fans.
- If you don't regularly use your entire house, use window AC units in your most frequented rooms, and only when you're in the room. Turn off the AC when you leave the room for more than 30 minutes.

What the Utility Companies Don't Tell You

Unless there's an energy shortage, they don't care if you run up your bill. However, you can reduce your bills and use your energy efficiently all the time. Here's how:

- A refrigerator eats 30 percent of the average electric bill. Make sure your door seal is keeping the chill in. Place a dollar bill against it, then close the door. If you can pull the bill out easily, replace the seal.
- About 40 percent of your home heating escapes outdoors due to poor insulation. Call your power company, not an insulation contractor, for an audit of your insulation situation.

Showerhead Alert!

It could be dripping with the deadly Legionnaires' disease. Between 8,000 and 18,000 people are diagnosed with it each year, and it kills up to 30 percent of those who contract it.

Legionella organisms are found in water systems, including household whirlpool spas and showerheads. While the common conception is that it erupts in large outbreaks, most cases are single and isolated.

Symptoms include fever, chills, cough, achy muscles, headache, and lethargy. Treatment: a routine course of antibiotics. Prevention: clean and disinfect water sources frequently.

■ Fluorescent bulbs last ten times longer than regular ones and use a quarter of the energy. They come in regular bulb shapes that screw into ordinary sockets.

■ Your biggest water expense is the toilet: six gallons per flush for a regular toilet, 1.6 for low-flush models. If your toilet is on old model, fill a couple half-gallon milk jugs with gravel and place them in your tank to displace the water, so that less is used with each flush. Also, install a flow restrictor on your showerhead.

What's in the Wood?

Actually it's in wood-based products, and here's the hint: It's a colorless, strong-smelling gas that can cause:

■ watery eyes
■ burning throat and sinuses
■ nausea
■ coughing
■ wheezing
■ skin rashes

Permanent-press, wrinkle-free, and polyester fabrics contain formaldehyde and will emit fumes. Wash these clothes before wearing them to avoid the largest level of exposure.

Here's the answer: formaldehyde. That's right. Besides pickling, it's used to hold the wood particles in your home entertainment center together.

Here's how to reduce or eliminate the formaldehyde in your life:

■ Buy pressed-wood products labeled "low-emitting." This is often called phenol-formaldehyde.

■ Increase ventilation when bringing new wood-based products into your home.

■ Go for solid woods.

■ Don't use foamed-in-place insulation, especially urea-formaldehyde foam products.

Someone's in the Kitchen

And he shouldn't be. Six million burglaries happen yearly. If you come face to face with a burglar:

■ Lie like a dog. "Oh, you're here to check for roaches. Look under the kitchen sink." Be cool. Don't let on that you know he's not the exterminator.

■ Don't stage a confrontation. Most burglars are there only to steal your stuff, not to harm you.

■ Pretend you're asleep.

The best way to avoid meeting a burglar is to lock your doors and windows. In half of all home break-ins, the burglar simply slips in through an unlocked window or an unlocked door.

Don't Do That in the Bedroom!

Hiding your valuables, that is. Thieves usually search

that room more thoroughly than any other. And don't stash them in the back of a drawer, either. That's the first place they look. Instead, hide your treasure in:

- an old book (hollow out the pages)
- a zippered couch cushion
- your pots and pans
- your freezer
- a generic food can

Hiding places in the attic, basement, or kitchen are the best. Kitchens are never touched in 90 percent of all burglaries.

Ten Things Every Burglar Loves

1. weak locks
2. easy-access sliding glass doors
3. unlocked windows and easy-to-pick window locks
4. basement windows without grilles or grates

Woof! Woof!

Burglars hate dogs—or even the hint of a dog.

Post "Beware of Dog" signs on your house. Don't tack them up where they can be observed from the street. If a burglar is watching your house and sees the sign, he can check out the dog situation to see if you're bluffing. Instead, use the element of surprise. Stick that sign above the door knob and on windows.

Buy a dog. Make sure Fido barks.

Leave a giant-size dog bowl in plain sight.

If you don't want a dog, buy or make a tape of a dog barking. Keep a tape recorder near your door and play it when you suspect trouble.

5. door keys in the usual places: under a mat, under a nearby conspicuous rock, or in a nearby flowerpot

6. unlocked or flimsy doors—and homes without security screen doors

7. no lights on inside the house

8. no security or motion-detector lights outside

9. mail and newspapers piled up when you're gone

10. no alarm system

Soapy Overkill

Antibacterial soaps are the best choice? Wrong! In fact, while you think you're getting cleaner by eliminating all those bacteria, you're actually setting yourself up to play host to even more. Why? Antibacterials, like antibiotics, lose their effectiveness when overused. Bacteria get real smart real fast and build up a resistance. The more agents used to kill them, the more they'll don their armor.

New Kid on the Block

Produce cleaning solutions are the latest rage, and slick advertising will have you believe that they get your fruits and vegetables cleaner than you can. Not true. According to recent government studies, water and some good, hard scrubbing do just as well. So before you plunk down a hefty chunk of change for a solution that is made up, mainly, of citric acid and baking soda, consider your other option: scrub for free and buy even more fruits and veggies.

Here's how to keep bacteria under control:

■ Use regular soap and water on hands and dishes.

Use ½ tsp of bleach per quart of water as a disinfectant.

Use antibacterial agents sparingly, such as when there's an illness in the house.

Do You Know Your Furnace?

It sits in your basement, garage, or closet burning at 1,200 degrees, so you should know something about it. For example:

How often should it be checked? Once a year.

The flame in your furnace should be what color? A bright, steady blue. If it isn't, or it flickers, get it checked.

■ Carbon monoxide levels in your home can *not* be detected by smell. CO is odorless. Symptoms of carbon monoxide poisoning are dizziness, headache, fatigue, and nausea. Carbon monoxide poisoning can be fatal. Buy a CO detector!

■ If you smell natural gas leaking from your furnace, you should *not* call for help. Using a phone can cause tiny electrical sparks that could ignite if they come in contact with the gas. Electric lights cause sparking, too, so don't turn them on, either.

It's Radioactive...

...and it's in your home. Smoke detectors contain a low level of radiation that isn't considered harmful to people. However, if they break, this radiation makes them a headache to throw away.

■ You shouldn't throw them in the trash.

■ Most hazardous-materials drop-off sites won't take them.

Your best bet is to get rid of the detector according to instructions on the package. Or:

- Wear disposable gloves, or stick your hand in a plastic zippy bag, when taking it off the ceiling.
- Seal it in the bag.
- Return it to the manufacturer with a note explaining that you're returning it for disposal.

Let's Play Telephone

Are you getting the best deal? Do you even know how to find it?

First, call all the major carriers. Tell them where and when you call the most and ask for a recommendation for the best plan. Then compare.

Most major companies have comparable offers, so concentrate on the special deals that would most benefit you:

- weekend savings
- frequent flyer miles
- free Fridays
- bills exactly what you use; doesn't round up to the next portion of a minute increment

Mix and match. Use a company with great long-distance day rates and, at night, a discount service such as one of those 10-10-whatever-the-number deals.

Ask for a better deal. Yes, you can do that. One of the most common bargaining points is the monthly base long-distance fee. Many phone companies will waive them.

Why Pay More?

You can make your phone number unlisted, but it will cost you several extra bucks a month. Forget that! You can get all the phone privacy you need for free by changing your listing to a different name:

Beware of the Prepaid Phone Card

It may seem like a good idea, but typical charges are two to three times more per minute. Typical complaints:

- Access numbers don't work.
- The card company goes out of business, leaving the holder with a useless card.
- Access and customer service numbers are constantly busy.
- There are hidden connection charges and taxes.

Better choice: Use a long-distance card from your phone carrier.

- your maiden name
- Fido's name
- Great-Grandma's name

The added bonus comes at dinnertime when the sales calls begin and someone starts off with, "How are you this evening, Mrs. Fido?" You can hang up before the second sentence is uttered.

Slam Dancing

Your long-distance carrier is strictly your choice, but there are no guarantees you'll remain with your chosen provider. Some phone companies "slam" customers from other phone companies, meaning they switch the telephone service of a competitor's customer over to their own company without permission or notification.

The only way you'll find out if you've been slammed is by reading your bill. It happens all the time, so if you like your long-distance carrier, call your phone company and ask them to put an anti-slam on your line. It's free.

CHAPTER 3

Secrets for Successful Living

Success makes you feel great, doesn't it? Even little successes, such as learning to dress sharply or improving your memory, can put a whole new spin on your life—as well as the way others perceive you. Try a few of these simple success tips and see what happens.

You're the Expert

Nothing spells success better than being an expert on something. It doesn't matter what, and it's not difficult to do. Here are some ways to join the distinguished ranks:

- Write an article for a magazine specializing in your field of expertise. If you're an expert on crappie fishing, there's a magazine just waiting for your information. Find a comprehensive listing of magazines in *Writer's Market* (Writer's Digest Books).

- Teach a continuing education course at your local college. You don't need a degree. Just call the continuing ed office and ask how.

- Attend conferences and seminars in your field of expertise, and rub elbows with other experts. Pass out business cards and distribute your "expert" resume.

What's Pea Green and Polyester?

The suit you *won't* buy, that's what. Here are some tips for buying a suit that makes you look like a million bucks' worth of success:

- Wool! It breathes, it wears well, and there never was a pea green wool suit.
- Style: These are all winners...

  - American cut: This is the typical everyday suit.

  - Full cut: This is not tapered at the waist and is a bit more roomy than other styles.

  - European cut: This tapers at the waist for a trim look.

- Color: Pick basic darks. Conservative pinstripes work well, too.
- Shirt: Select plain white or blue. Conservative stripes are classy, also.
- Tie: Choose one that matches your shirt. Don't wear a striped tie with a striped shirt!
- Accessories: Your belt should match your shoes, and each should be leather. Your socks must match your pants.

- Never, ever mix blacks and browns!

And This for the Ladies

You get your turn at success when it comes to your attire, too.

- In terms of color, go universal: black, white, gray, navy.
- Wear your hair back in a professional style, and make sure your nails are neat and clean.
- Wear minimal makeup and jewelry.
- Purse and shoes should match.
- Wear neutral, skin-tone hose without any runs.

I Do *What* With This Fork?

You're at a lavish dinner party and the food looks delicious, but there's one obstacle stopping you from digging in—the utensils. Which of your forks was

The Manners That Got Away

Our mothers taught us, but we forgot. Today, it seems as if traditional manners aren't as important as they were 50 years ago. But manners do count where real success is concerned. Here are some oldies but goodies:

- Return phone calls (and e-mails) within 48 hours.
- Write a response to a letter within two weeks.
- Thank you notes aren't just for gifts. They're also for favors, meals, and other acts of kindness.

meant for lettuce, and which is the one for beef? Here's how to succeed at the dinner table:

- Use your utensils from the outside in, in the order in which the food is served.

- Never let your utensils touch the table once they've been used; they'll dirty the tablecloth. Leave them on, or lean them against, the right rim of the plate.

- Spoon your soup away from you and sip it from the side of the spoon. When you're finished, remove the spoon from

the cup and place it on the saucer underneath.

Mastering the Back Massage

Your success here will reap untold rewards in the personal relationship department. Here are five basic massage moves that never fail:

1. Start with a little oil, then place palms flat on both sides of the spine, just above the hips. Move up and over the shoulders, then along the rib cage. (Warning: Never massage the spine.)

2. Move your hand in circles, away from the spine, then back, using your left hand for a few circles and then your right. Don't stop the flow of motion.

3. Knead the muscles, but not in the neck or over the ribs.

4. Rake the fleshy part of your fingers over the entire massaged area.

5. End with a feathery touch, lightly tapping every place you massaged.

Tidy It Up

A mess never conveys success. If you live in one, that clutter is making you inefficient. So here are a few ways to unclutter successfully:

■ Follow the one-a-day rule: either one room per day or one hour every day. Small, manageable tasks won't overwhelm you.

■ Start with the least cluttered room first, then work your way to the most cluttered. This way, you won't get frustrated at the beginning of your chore.

■ Make three piles:

 • what you use all the time

 • what you haven't used or worn in a year

 • what you haven't used in two years

■ Then organize into these categories:

 • keepers

 • throwaways

 • giveaways

 • can't decide (this stuff goes into storage)

Worm Your Way Out of a Traffic Ticket

This is where your success could save you some big bucks. So try one, or a combination of several, of these techniques to get out of that ticket:

■ Good attitude. Officers don't receive too many

Cop Bait

When you're pulled over, these are the traffic ticket decision-makers that go against you:

- red car
- tinted windows
- dents, broken windows, rust
- trash in the car
- anything other than parking tags hanging from the rearview mirror, and that includes those fuzzy dice

pleasant reactions in a day, and yours may be the one that counts.

Humor. Laugh about it as you apologize. Tell a joke or funny story about someone else's traffic ticket experience.

Conversation. Silence implies something to hide.

Honesty. "I screwed up, officer. I'm sorry." The truth probably won't get you off the hook, but it could get your fine reduced.

Crying. Tears bring on sympathy, unless they're from a man.

Spotting a Liar

No two liars lie alike, and sometimes it's difficult for even the experts to sort truth from fiction. But here are a few clues that may help you spot a big, fat liar:

- stuttering or stammering
- strained or high-pitched voice
- evasive words or answers
- too many nonwords: ah...uh...
- nervous gestures or a marked lack of gestures

- the flash of a facial expression followed by an instant cover-up

Big tip: Liars do slip up, especially under stress. If you think someone is lying to you, observe her closely, listen carefully, and remember every detail of the conversation. Ask questions that will cause the liar to repeat herself, then listen for changes or inconsistencies in the story.

A Little on the Sly Side?

Maybe, but every successful sleuth knows how to get just a little more information out of someone.

- Use frequent, long pauses. People respond by filling in the gaps.

- Come up with some responsive facial gestures: arching an eyebrow, frowning, smiling, or looking startled or surprised. Make sure you whip out your expressions on the right cue, though.

- Be supportive: "You're kidding!" "I certainly agree!" "Exactly!" "I know what you mean." Also nod or shake your head when appropriate.

- Ask casual questions at the right time. "Why?" "How did that happen?"

- Draw comparisons: "Something like that happened to me."

You Must Remember This

And if you don't, here are some tricks to turn that lackluster memory into a success story:

- Go over the important stuff just before you go to sleep.

Break up information into pieces—a little here and a little there.

Write down what he said. Read it later. Seeing is remembering.

Repeat it—aloud.

Tie it to something you do remember.

And to remember names:

Note everything about the person: mannerisms, speech patterns, dress.

Repeat the name after she's said it, as a means of confirmation.

Think about the name several times over the next few hours, and visualize the person who was attached to it.

Take It to Your Own People's Court

It's a simple procedure, and the key to success in small claims court is knowing the way it works.

■ Every jurisdiction has a dollar limit for lawsuits. Know yours.

■ Every jurisdiction has a time limit for filing suit. Don't exceed yours.

■ Prove your claim: documents, witnesses, photos. Written statements, notarized or not, rarely work.

■ Can you actually collect? Judges hate trials that are just someone's way to get their day in court. Don't go to court just for a moral victory.

■ Prepare your presentation beforehand. Be precise, accurate, and to the point. Start with the end of the story first, then go back and pick up the main points: "Due to Mr. Smith's negligence, I spent three days in the hospital. Here's what happened..."

■ Dress up. You're the lawyer, and no successful lawyer ever won a case while wearing dirty jeans.

Willy Billy and Roy Bob

They don't sound like names attached to too much success, do they? If your parents stuck you with a moniker disaster, you can dump it. Here's how:

- Pick a name and use it. This is called common usage. It's official, but to put a stamp of legitimacy on it, all you have to do is to acquire and fill out a name change form from the Social Security office. In a matter of days, your common usage name will have your legal Social Security number attached to it.

- File it in court. It's a matter of paperwork, fees, and sometimes a brief appearance before the judge. However, you don't need a lawyer. Call your city clerk and ask how to get the name-change ball rolling.

Brighten That Sr

Can you think of anything that beams success more than a mouth full of white teeth? Here are the ways you can brighten your smile:

- Get bleached by your dentist. You'll sit in the chair for about an hour, with your mouth jammed full of gel, and you'll pay some hefty dollars. However, you'll get results that should last for several years.

- Buy an over-the-counter kit. It will take several weeks to achieve the results you want, but the cost is affordable. *Don't do it until you check with your tooth doc, though.* The mouth tray you'll use isn't a custom fit, and it can cause serious gum irritation.

- Hit a happy medium. Have your dentist make your mouth tray, then do the rest at home.

Scam Alert!

"I was driving by when I noticed that your roof is sagging. I just happen to have some roofing materials in my truck, and I wouldn't feel right leaving here knowing your old roof could collapse any minute." Nearly one in five Americans have been scammed. Are you about to join the ranks?

Meet Mr. Con Man

He's not necessarily the loud, brash, can't-take-no-for-an-answer guy in the plaid suit you'd expect. He's well dressed, appears to have a connection with someone important, and has a story that can tug at your heart. He's also a she, working her way through college or trying to support her three children after her husband's death.

And both Mr. and Ms. Con are persuasive, concerned for your welfare and eager to do *anything* to help you, including offering you that once-in-a-lifetime deal that will get them fired if the boss finds out.

Mr. Con Checklist

You suspect he's not honest, but you're just not sure. Apply the con man test: If any of the following situations arise, don't go any further.

- He insists upon secrecy concerning his deal.
- Cash only; no checks.

FAST FACT

What's the con gender? The guys have it, at 90 to 95 percent.

But I'm a Little Short of Cash

"No problem. I know someone who can make you a great deal on a loan." Many contractors have a ready-to-go loan broker who either offers sky-high interest rates or offers to "hold" the deed until the costs of the work are paid off. Either way, you risk losing your house or staying forever in debt. If you're short of cash, find your own loan. Start with your personal lending institution.

- You must pay before the service is completed.
- You have to make the deal right now—or lose out.
- You've done a complete turn-around from your original decision.
- You're handing over money you hadn't intended to.
- He told you he's more interested in helping you than making money.

The Great Home Repair Rip-off

Thirty-two percent of all consumers aged 50 to 64 say they've been swindled in a home repair deal. What's the tip-off that you're about to be taken? Simple: The home repair huckster shows up on your doorstep without you ever calling him.

To protect yourself:

- Never talk to anyone you didn't call.
- Don't fall for one-day-only bargains.
- Check with your Better Business Bureau before you agree to anything.
- Ask for references, then check them.
- Ask about other jobs in progress, then do a drive-by inspection.
- Get other estimates, in writing.

- Don't agree to payment in full before the job is finished.
- Don't sign a contract or any papers you don't understand.
- Get everything in writing. Have him spell out all details.

Top Five Home Repair Scammers

1. Mr. Johnny on the Spot: He'll be on your doorstep ten minutes after a natural disaster, ready to do whatever it takes to help you. His price will be the next natural disaster you'll face.

2. Mrs. Show Me More Money: She doesn't have enough moolah to do the job, and when you advance what she needs, you won't have to worry about her finishing the job. She won't. She'll be gone.

3. Mr. Just in the Neighborhood and his partner, Mr. Leftover Materials: They'll offer a cheap deal because they already have the materials, and you'll get what you pay for: cheap (unless the third partner is Mr. Take the Money and Run, in which case you won't get anything).

4. Mrs. Free Test: She'll test your home for radon, termites, or rats, and guess what? You've got 'em! And isn't it amazing that right this very minute she has what she needs to get rid of whatever you have?

5. Mr. Better Do It Right: He'll bamboozle you with other costly projects that have to be fixed first.

The Scam Delivery Man

He comes right to your door, just like the guy who brings the pizza. He targets people who spend a lot of time at home, or who live alone, and he sells everything from vacuum cleaners to pots and pans to graves.

First rule: Don't let him in.

Second rule: Tell him he can't come in.

If he gets in anyway, then...

- Don't buy on impulse.
- If you like the product, ask to see his credentials.
- Tell him you'll think about it, and ask for his phone number so you can contact him when you've decided.
- Don't sign a contract until you've thought about it for a day or two.

Cooling Down

That Joy of Taxidermy kit isn't what you thought it would be, so what can you do? If you bought it in your home, and paid more than $25, the Federal Trade Commission's Cooling Off Rule will get you off the hook. Take note:

- Legitimate door-to-door sales contracts come with two cancellation forms. Sign and date one, then mail it to the address on the form. Keep the other copy.
- You can change your mind about the deal for up to 72 hours, so get that form in the mail before midnight of the third business day. (Saturday is a business day, too.)
- Use certified mail so that you will have proof of delivery.

After you cancel, the seller must refund your money within ten days. Let him pick up that taxidermy kit, though. You aren't required to ship it back. If he doesn't, it's yours to keep, free.

For more information, call 877-FTC-HELP or visit www.ftc.gov.

Don't Bet the Bank on This One

A "bank examiner" calls to tell you that something suspicious is going on with your account. He wants to catch that thieving bank teller in the act, but he needs your help. Here's the rest of the swindle:

You're asked to withdraw some money from your account—$500 to several thousand dollars.

The examiner says he will take your money and mark the bills so that the teller can be caught with them, red-handed.

You'll be offered a reward for your help.

You're told you'll get your money back, and the marked bills will be entered as evidence.

Bye-bye money.

What to do:

Hang up if you get the call.

Report the incident to your bank manager.

Call the police.

Alms for the Poor

Upward of 10 percent of the more than $100 billion given to charity every year goes to line the pockets of a phony philanthropist. He calls and pleads for money to send an underprivileged child to camp, but the only camp that money sees is Camp You've Just Been Had.

Here are the big charity rip-off tip-offs:

■ They can't wait for you to mail a check. They'll be at your door in 20 minutes.

■ They won't send you a brochure about the charity.

■ They won't give you specifics about the charity, especially not a mailing address or phone number.

Here's what you should do:

■ Contact your Better Business Bureau to see if the charity is legitimately registered.

■ Check your charity's credentials with:

1. American Institute of Philanthropy
4905 Del Ray Ave., Suite 300W

Putting Out the Fire

They come in the guise of a police officer or firefighter, because you're generous with those who put their lives on the line to serve and protect. But beware. Police and fire fund-raising scams abound. Any fund-raising organization that's on the up-and-up will be glad to wait until you can check them out, and they'll give you the information you need to do so. Flimflam police and firefighter charities won't give you anything, so call the real police if the flimflam man calls you.

Bethesda, MD 20814
301-913-5200
www.charitywatch.org

2. National Charities Information Bureau
19 Union Square West
New York, NY 10003
212-929-6300
www.give.org

Smooth Operator

Urgent! Call this number to find out about:

■ your prize

■ the trip you've just won

■ the dead uncle you didn't know you had

If you don't recognize the number, you could be calling a phone fraud with an account that bills you up to $10 a minute for every minute you talk. And the person on the other end of the line knows just how to keep you talking.

Many phone frauds operate in countries that give kickbacks for using foreign phone services. Chances are you're being set up if the area code you're asked to call is any of the following: 664 (Montserrat), 758 (St. Lucia), 809 (Dominican Republic), or 011-(international access code).

Look Out for These Rogue Area Codes, Too!

These are less-used but nonetheless rip-off area codes:

264 Anguilla

268 Antigua and Barbuda

242 Bahamas

246 Barbados

441 Bermuda

284 British Virgin Islands

245 Cayman Islands

767 Dominica

473 Grenada

876 Jamaica

869 St. Kitts and Nevis

784 St. Vincent/Grenadines

868 Trinidad and Tobago

The beauty of these area codes, for the thief, is that they appear to be in the United States, and most people won't suspect they're really dialing into a high, foreign telephone-charge area.

Guess Who's Coming to Dinner

You're about to take a bite of that delicious roast when suddenly *ding-a-ling!*

There are an estimated 14,000 fraudulent telemarketing operations dragging in $40 billion every year, and they've got your number because:

■ You can't tell, over the phone, if your caller is legitimate.

■ You're too polite to hang up. Swindlers know that and use it to their advantage.

■ You want to believe that a too-good-to-be-true offer can really happen to you.

Even though telephone tricksters are hard to catch, telemarketing fraud is a crime, punishable by imprisonment. Here's how to know if that dinner caller is legitimate:

About Those PINs

The easy numbers for a thief to pick out are:

- addresses
- birth dates
- Social Security numbers
- telephone numbers
- the numerical equivalent of your name
- obvious sequences: 1,2,3,4 or 2,4,6,8 or 0,0,0,0

Keep your PINs random. Change them at least twice a year. Don't write them on bank or credit cards, and don't keep them on your person or in your purse or car. And, when you're standing at a bank machine, block all views of your transaction. Ask the person behind you to step back if she's too close. If she won't, allow her to go ahead of you.

■ Ask for a call-back number so you can check out the deal.

■ If she refuses, or gives you that old "make a decision now or the deal's off" line, it's a fraud.

Call the National Fraud Information Center (NFIC) at 800-876-7060 for more information on telemarketing fraud.

Is Your Loved One Getting Scammed?

Rip-off artists target their victims well, and they don't usually leave a trace. But there are subtle signs that your loved one is a victim.

■ He gets frequent calls offering valuable awards.

■ She's making more charitable contributions than usual.

- His bank statements show more transactions than usual, especially to out-of-state companies.
- She's very secretive about her phone calls and financial transactions.
- He's having sudden financial trouble—unable to pay bills or buy food.

Swindlers stress the need for absolute secrecy concerning their deal, so if you think there's a fraud afoot, don't threaten to take away your loved one's financial independence. This could cause her to become more secretive. Instead, call your local consumer protection agency or the NFIC.

Your Number's Up

Make sure your credit card number's up only when *you* use it. Here's how:

- At the checkout, keep your card hidden from the view of others.
- Don't dump your receipts in a public trash can. Be aware that, if you live in certain apartment or condo buildings, your personal trash winds up in a public Dumpster—fresh pickin's for sneaky crooks.
- Never give your credit card number to a telemarketer.
- Check monthly statements for anything you didn't purchase. Check them against your receipts, too.
- Never leave blank spaces where amounts can be added later. If there is a line for a tip, for instance, either enter an amount or draw a line through the space.
- When in doubt, call your credit card company.

FAST FACT

Thinking about buying something online? Search the Better Business Bureau's online site at www.bbbonline.org to make sure your cyber store is legitimate.

Online Security

Most cyber shops are honest about protecting your credit card number when you enter it in an online purchase. But there are hackers out there who can get that number no matter how well it's cyber protected. If you like shopping from a monitor, call in your credit card number and ask that it's not stored for future use. Or find out how you can send a check; most cyber vendors will accept checks.

Make Some *Real* Money

Medicare is ready to place its bucks on the line to pay you if you find someone trying to cheat them. So if you know someone who's on the shady side when it comes to Uncle Sam's dollars for the elderly and disabled, obtain a copy of "Fraud and Abuse" from www.medicare.gov—or call 800-447-8477 for a copy. Then learn how to spot fraud and claim that reward.

CHAPTER 5

Buying on the Cheap

Bargain-smart shoppers know there are always ways to make better deals, no matter what they're buying. Sometimes it's just a matter of asking, while other times it's knowing what the salesperson isn't telling you. So do you want to know a few bargain secrets? Read on.

Buzzzzzz!

For salespeople, it's all in the wording. Words entice, seduce, and cement a sale. Here are a few of those deal-making buzzwords:

- "Company policy." Don't believe it. Policies were made to be negotiated, and company policies are never set in stone when there's money to be made.

- "Sale." Is it really? The term "sale" is often a come-on used to lure a customer into a store. If you're buying a big-bucks sales item, check to see if it's really a sale by asking to see proof of its regular price.

- "Low maintenance." It's a come-on term, too. "Low" depends on your definition of how much time and effort you care to invest in maintenance.

- "Limited warranty." "Limited" usually means a lot *less* warranty than a lot more.

Grocery Grabbing

It's a supermarket jungle out there, and that jungle's not very friendly. Here are some tips that will help you swing from aisle to aisle a little easier:

- The best sales, called loss-leaders, are listed on the front and back of the flyers.
- All bunches are not equal. When buying by the bunch, stick it on the scale to find the weightiest.
- Check out those unit prices on the shelf tag, even if you have to carry a magnifying glass. Common thinking is that buying in larger quantities is cheaper, but that's not necessarily so.
- Look for those sale bins of about-to-be-tossed items,

FAST FACT

Those delicious-smelling fresh foods in your grocery store's hot foods section can be twice the cost of ones you fix at home. On the other hand, grocery store meals can be half the cost of restaurant fare.

and ask the department manager for a better deal.

Wrong Line Again?

Listen up! Here are ways to spot the movers from the slackers:

- Don't select your cashier at random. Watch for one who's speedy and efficient, then search for that cashier every time you shop.
- Find a line with a bagger. In a store that scans groceries, a bagger will increase the line speed by 100 percent.
- Avoid anyone with a tag that says "Trainee."
- Watch the carts:
  - Those with identical items are faster because scanning can be done in groups, not as single items.
  - Beware of produce shoppers. Each bag of parsnips and rutabagas has to be weighed.

- Look out for check cashers. It takes time to write and verify checks. Debit and credit card users slow the line, too.

Something Smells Fishy

Beware of the fresh fish you buy. It may not be the fresh catch you'd hoped it would be. Here are some ways to spot the freshest catch:

- Eyes are clear and bulging.
- Flesh is firm and shiny.
- Gills are bright red and without slime.
- Flesh springs back when you press it.
- Smell is mild, not fishy or ammonia-like.

And about that fish you order in the restaurant: It's ordered fresh for the weekend, which means skip the fish on those early days of the week. What you'll get will be what wasn't consumed on Friday, Saturday, and Sunday.

Scrod Secret

Scrod isn't a type of fish. It's a term that originated in Boston and was used to describe the catch of the day. It also describes any fish under 2½ pounds. So when you order or buy scrod, you're really getting cod, haddock, or pollock.

To Everything There Is a Season

A time to sow and a time to reap the best seasonal sales bargains:

- January: appliances, books, carpets, and toys
- February: air conditioners, silverware, storm windows, TVs, and winter clothing
- March: garden supplies, housewares, and luggage
- April: fabric, hosiery, and lingerie
- May: jewelry, outdoor furniture, rugs, and tires

June: bedding, floor covering, men's clothing, and sleepwear

July: electronic equipment, furniture, men's shoes, and summer clothing

August: carpeting, curtains, electric fans, and tires

September: bicycles, cars (outgoing models), garden equipment, lamps, and paint

October: cars (outgoing models), fall clothing, fishing gear, and major appliances

November: blankets, used cars, men's suits, and shoes

December: after-Christmas cards and wrapping paper, cruise wear, coats, and hats

More Bargains!

Huge discounts are waiting—if you know where to find them. Here are some tips:

■ Those clothes on the 70-percent-off rack aren't always there because they're damaged goods. They may be mis-sized; try them on. Often they're just way past their season, and stores do not stockpile seasonal items.

■ You know that beautifully decorated artificial Christmas tree you see every time you walk into your favorite store? It's for sale, usually at a pretty good discount, after Christmas. But you don't have to wait until Santa slides back up your chimney to make the deal. Grab the store manager and do your after-Christmas shopping well before Christmas.

■ If you live near a vacation spot, wait until the tourist season is over to buy items associated with the area, such as swimsuits and ski supplies. When the tourist season dries up, those things may be reduced up to 75 percent.

Come On Down, the Price Is Better!

It's usually a hush-hush deal, but most stores will match or even top the competition's price. Here's the best way to go about price matching:

- Call several stores to check the price of what you're buying.
- Ask if they price match.
- Ask if they pay 10 percent of the difference, too. Many stores do.
- Go to the most expensive store that also gives the 10-percent difference. Buy your item there.
- Have them price check the least expensive store.

You'll get the lower price, plus 10 percent of the difference between the highest and lowest prices.

Down, But Not Out

If you get ripped off on any consumer deal, here's what to do:

- Talk to the manager. Try to resolve the issue. Ask for a refund.
- If you don't get satisfaction, make your requests known to those at the next level up. Keep climbing until you find someone who will listen or has the power to resolve the issue.
- This next step is very important: Let them know you intend to win—and where you'll take the issue if you have to. Don't threaten with an attorney; they know that most people don't hire an attorney to straighten out con-

FAST FACT

Be careful if you intend to buy something from one of those stores that's always going out of business. Many such stores overinflate their asking price so they can lower it enough to make an unsuspecting shopper believe she's getting a great close-out deal.

sumer problems because the cost is too high. Tell the person who's ripping you off that you will file a complaint with your local Better Business Bureau, then with the attorney general's consumer division in your state. Then do it.

■ If your local television station has a consumer hotline, give them a ring.

■ If the dollar amount in question is high, consider taking your case to small claims court.

Beware the Gouging Pay Phone!

Most pay phones are owned by local phone companies. There are some, though, that are customer-owned, currency-operated telephones (COCOT), and they team up with alternative operator services (AOS) to pluck every last penny out of your pockets. The result can be services priced ten times more than those offered by a standard long-distance carrier. Here's the rest you need to know:

■ To find out if you're using a regular provider instead of a COCOT, check for a telephone company logo.

■ Don't use a calling card. An AOS often adds a sky-high surcharge.

■ Bypass the AOS by dialing your primary carrier's equal-access code.

Let Your Fingers Do the Shopping

Online shopping is popular these days, and for the most part it's convenient. However, you've got to be smart about it. Here's how:

■ Check out the seller with the Online Better Business Bureau or the attorney general of the state in which the seller is based.

■ Protect your privacy. Provide as little private information as possible.

■ Guard your passwords.

- Pay by credit card. It offers the most consumer protection.
- Use a secure server. You'll know the site is secured when you see a closed padlock or unbroken key symbol. This symbol can usually be found in the bottom left corner of your screen.
- Print the details of your transaction.

And remember: When in doubt, don't do it.

Better Brew Bargains

Beer makes up 88 percent of all alcohol sold, and over half of what's sold comes from only three breweries. But in the booze world, beer is inexpensive and takes up a lot of shelf space, and retailers don't want to keep it around long. So, here's how to get some brewski bargains:

- Buy your beer in the summer, when it's cheapest.
- Store it in a cool, dark place, and don't move it until you drink it because jostling makes it go flat. Beer will keep for six months, so you can stock up for your next Super Bowl party in August, when prices are down.
- Don't buy into the "beautiful people" advertising hype. Those designer brands can cost up to 50

Phantom of the Auction

Someone just outbid you, and you didn't see who it was. Maybe that's because it wasn't a "who" but instead the auction house phantom. One of the oldest auction ploys in the book is for the "house" to bid against eager bidders in order to drive up their bids. In other words, the phantom is really a case of the auctioneer pretending someone has upped the bid when, in fact, he's done it himself.

percent more than your common everyday suds.

Beating the Flea Deal

There are *always* better flea market deals to be made. Here are some tips:

- Bargain down, regardless of the asking price. Discounts of 10 percent are standard, but if the dealer really needs a sale, you could get 20 to 30 percent off. So start with an offer of at least 25 percent less.

- Don't seem eager. Eager means a smaller discount because the dealer knows you really want it and are probably willing to pay more.

- Pass up anything that doesn't have a price tag. Many dealers prefer to make arbitrary price decisions based on your interest and appearance, which means you could be paying more for it than the guy behind you would.

CHAPTER 6 Vital Health Secrets

Though we spend billions of dollars each year on our health, it's often a keep-your-fingers-crossed kind of proposition. Are they telling us everything? That's a hard one to answer, especially since nowadays you can't throw a rock without hitting yet another source offering medical advice or information—from billboards to the Internet. This chapter, however, includes interesting health-wise tidbits you probably haven't heard.

A Pound on the Hips

Don't believe the diet ads. People are not putting on five to ten pounds between Thanksgiving and New Year's Day. That's just a line to get you to buy their diet products. Studies actually show that the average holiday weight gain is about a pound. Here are a few other weighty facts:

- More than half of all adult Americans are overweight —about 51 percent of all women and 60 percent of all men.

- Eleven percent of all children aged 6 to 17 are overweight.

- Americans gain an average of one pound for every year of their adult life.

- During the 1990s, obesity increased in every state, in both genders, and across all ethnicities, age groups, and educational levels.

- Americans spend more than $33 billion annually on weight-loss products.

Take This and Divide It by That

The degree to which you're overweight, or underweight, is best measured not by the reading on a scale but by your body mass index, or BMI. To determine yours, take your weight in kilograms and divide it by your height in meters, then square it. Got it? If not, go to www.nhlbisupport.com/bmi/bmicalc.htm and plug in the right numbers. And don't cheat. No one's peeking. If your BMI is 25 to 29.9, you're overweight. Thirty or above is considered obese.

The Rest of the Story

That extra holiday pound wouldn't be so bad if we stuck to our New Year's resolution to get rid of it, but we don't. Instead, we fill up the bowl with chips, grab a six-pack, and lie back to watch the game. And here's the result:

- Only 22 percent of adult Americans exercise regularly (five times a week for 30 minutes).

- About 15 percent get the recommended amount of vigorous physical activity (three times a week for 20 minutes).

- About 25 percent report no physical activity at all, which is the same number in young people aged 12 to 21.

Leg Lumps and Bottom Bumps

In spite of what the ads say, cellulite is plain old fat dressed up with a fancy name in order to rake in a fat wad of money. These are some of the cellulite cure-alls that are really cure-nothings:

- Electrical muscle stimulators. They're for relaxing muscles and increasing blood circulation.

- Iontophoresis devices. They're for diagnosing cystic fibrosis.
- Body wrap. This causes only a temporary water loss from perspiration.
- Oral agents. No study proves that popping a pill is a cellulite remedy.

Then there's endodermologie, a massager that compresses cellulite tissue. It works—to the tune of $55 per treatment, with 20 needed to achieve the best result and two maintenance treatments per month thereafter. Average change in body circumference is just over six-tenths of an inch. And it's not permanent. Once you stop the treatment, that dimpled look returns.

All Chicken Isn't Equal

In fact, some parts are fattier than beef. Here are the chicken facts you should know:

- Chicken has 1½ times more fat than turkey.
- Skinless thighs are twice as fatty as skinless drumsticks.
- A four-ounce chunk of skinless chicken thigh has more fat than four ounces of trimmed round steak, sirloin, and pork tenderloin.
- Wings are fattier than drumsticks, while backs are fattier than thighs.

Sniff Away Those Pounds

Your brain's olfactory bulb, where aromas are processed, is linked to your hunger control center. A nice, deep whiff of your favorite food may cross-wire the signals and trick your hunger controls into thinking you've been fed. The stronger the odor, the better. And go for hot foods. Heat revs up the smell.

■ Three and a half ounces of skinless dark meat has ten grams of fat, but a skinless breast has three grams.

And about that turkey: Self-basters are higher in fat than others because they're injected with fat to keep them moist.

Kung Pao No-No

Chinese food may be third on America's list of favorite foods, and 52 percent of us do believe it's more healthful than a usual diet, but look out!

■ An average Chinese dinner contains more sodium than we should eat in an entire day.

■ That typical Chinese meal also contains 70 percent of a day's fat allotment, 80 percent of an average day's cholesterol intake, and half of a day's saturated fat.

Here are some of the worst offenders:

■ egg roll
■ moo shu pork
■ kung pao chicken
■ sweet & sour pork
■ beef with broccoli
■ orange beef
■ hot & sour soup
■ lo mein
■ fried rice

FAST FACT

To make any Chinese food entree a healthier dish, mix one cup of it with one cup of steamed rice. This reduces the overall fat and sodium levels.

There's No Cure

But there are some things that can help you avoid getting the common cold.

■ Wash your hands often, especially after contact with someone who has a cold. Germs are most often transmitted by touch.

- You won't catch a cold from bad weather, since colds come from viruses. However, dressing appropriately will mean your body won't have to waste energy and resources keeping warm.

- Avoid overwork and stress. They also weaken the body's immune system.

And at the first sign of a cold, cut out dairy products, including ice cream. They increase mucus production, which makes breathing more difficult.

There's No Cure for Hangovers, Either

But you can ease the sharp thump of a hangover if you understand the chemistry. Here are the two basic facts:

- Consuming alcohol causes dehydration.

- The sick-feeling hangover that starts when the intoxi-cation ends results from your body's lack of proper fluid balance.

Here are a few things that could help:

- Don't drink on an empty stomach.

- Don't drink when you're tired.

- Tank up on nonalcoholic liquids immediately after you've finished drinking.

- Pop that aspirin or ibuprofen before you go to sleep.

- Switch to a lighter-colored liquor. The darker the booze, the worse the hangover.

The Best Test Available

Every year, 185,000 men are diagnosed with prostate cancer, and 40,000 will die because of it. There's a test available that decreased prostate cancer deaths by 16 percent in the 1990s, but you've got to ask for it because many doctors still aren't prescribing it. Here are some facts about the prostate-specific antigen (PSA) test:

- It's done by drawing blood from your arm, not your prostate.
- PSAs should be started when you're in your 40s or 50s and repeated yearly.

To get the most accurate results:

- Don't ejaculate for two days prior to the test.
- Get your PSA done before your rectal exam.
- If you're taking Propecia or Proscar, remind your doctor.

Exercises That Hurt You

Some of the old tried-and-true standards may not be as good for you as you think. But here's what you can do to make them safer:

- Sit-ups: These c̶ your back in d̶ sit all the way up. In̶ lie with your knees bent and cross your arms over your chest. Press your lower back into the floor and lift only your head, shoulders, and upper back.
- Double leg lifts: These also could strain your back. Instead, extend one leg and flat-foot the other on the floor. Raise your extended leg only six inches.
- Toe touches: These could cause back and knee strain—and even fainting. Instead, sit on the floor with one leg extended, one bent, and reach along your extended leg until you feel a gentle muscle stretch.

What's That? A Free, At-Home Hearing Test?

Here's how to check your hearing for free over the phone:

- Call 800-222-3277, 9 A.M. to 5 P.M. EST, Monday through Friday.
- Ask for a Dial-A-Hearing Screening Test number in your area.
- Call the number from a quiet room on a corded phone.
- Listen for four tones in each ear. If you don't hear a total of eight, you may wish to consult an audiologist.

Best of the Best-Kept Secrets

These medical tidbits could save you time, money, pain, and perhaps your life:

- Best doctor appointment time: First of the day.
- Doctor appointment day: Never on a Monday, when all the ailments of the weekend will arise.
- Fastest emergency room response: Arrive in an ambulance.
- Finding a doctor: Ask a friend.
- Letting your doctor know exactly what's wrong: Write it down and take it with you.
- Getting copies of your medical records: Just ask.
- Need a better price? Just ask. The fees for your doctor's services are negotiable, but you'll have to go straight to your doctor and not the billing department. They can't make that decision. And don't expect a fee adjustment from labs, hospitals, or other medical providers. Those prices are set in stone.
- Taking an iron supplement: Take vitamin C with it to increase absorption into the body.
- Understanding more about your medication: Ask your pharmacist.
- When your prescription runs out: Ask your pharmacist to call for a new order.

All About Your Drugs

Want to know more than you already do?

- For new drugs on the market, check them out with the Food and Drug Administration at www.fda.gov.

- For drugs you're already taking, check out www.CBShealthwatch.com.

- For free medications if you qualify, visit the Pharmaceutical Research and Manufacturers of America at www.phrma.org. Click on the Publications section and access Directory of Prescripti... Patient Assis... grams.

Going Onli... ...of to the Pharmacy?

Most pharmacy Web sites are on the up and up, but some aren't. Here are some buying tips:

- Check the National Association of Boards of Pharmacy at www.nabp.org or call 847-698-6227 to see if an online pharmacy is licensed and in good standing.

Before You Buy the Whole Prescription

That medication is new to you, and it's probably pretty costly. Since you've never taken it before, you may not want to plunk down your life's savings until you know you won't have an adverse reaction. So...

- Ask your physician for free samples so that you can make sure the drug will work for you.

- If your doctor doesn't have samples, ask your pharmacist to fill only two or three days' worth of the prescription first.

Now You've Haired It All

Hair analysis is the latest scam.

It will determine your general state of nutrition. Not!

An analysis will prediagnose the diseases you might get in the future. No way!

A quick test will determine the kind of diet/mineral/vitamin supplements you should take. Yeah, right!

Here's what the hair analyzers do:

Yank a hunk of hair.

Sell you a lotion, potion, or pill.

Stay away if the pharmacy will sell without a prescription or offers an online questionnaire as a means of prescribing a drug.

Do business only if a real, live pharmacist is available to answer questions.

Avoid foreign pharmacy sites. Their drug standards may differ from those in the U.S.

Check prices. They're not always as competitive as the advertising claims.

Free Tests!

And you don't even have to study for them. Every year, dozens of medical institutions conduct tests for people with certain conditions. Everything's free—physical exam, medications—and sometimes you even earn a stipend. To find out more, visit www.ClinicalTrials.gov or call 888-346-3656. Before you agree to anything:

- Check with your own physician.
- Ask these questions:

- Reason for this study?

- How long will the trial last?

- What's involved in the tests?

- Who will cover medical costs for side effects?

- How many trips to the doctor or hospital?

- Will I be hospitalized? How long?

Making the Stay a Little Cheaper

Unless you don't mind paying $4 for a can of soda, continue reading. Here are some of the take-alongs that will cost you a bunch if the hospital charges for them:

- personal toiletries, such as toothpaste, toothbrush, deodorant

- tissues

- lotion

- soft drinks

- snacks

- some over-the-counter medications, such as acetaminophen or antacids

Also, you may be allowed to take your own prescription drugs if they have nothing to do with the reason for which you're in the hospital—such as birth control pills when you're in for knee surgery. You'll have to get your doctor to write an order if you want to provide your own drugs.

FAST FACT

Is your insurance company pushing you out the hospital doors sooner than you think they should? Appeal the decision, in writing, immediately. They'll probably let you keep your bed until the decision is made. The decision will happen quicker than anything you've ever experienced in the healthcare system.

What They Know About You

Unfortunately, your private medical records aren't private. Insurance companies and marketers can get them. Anyone in a hospital, including the janitor, can access patient files if they have the know-how. Here are a few safeguards that will help keep your private matters a little more private:

- When filling out *any* form for *anyone*, volunteer as little personal information as possible.

FAST FACT

Doctors make a lot of money off self-referrals. This means that when they prescribe a test, they might send you to a lab in which they have part-ownership. A self-referral facility is usually more expensive, so check it out first, especially if you're making a co-payment.

- Ask your physician not to disclose information about you without your written permission.

- See if your medical records are included in your company personnel file. If the company has no formal policy about keeping medical records, ask to have yours expunged.

Even More Ways They Get That Information

They're sneaky, and they're good at it. Here are a few more ways they get to know you—and what you can do about it:

- Your medical records become available if you participate in company-sponsored programs, such as counseling. They may say they'll keep quiet, but there's no law that requires it. Make a request, in writing, that all records remain private, and get their agreement in writing. Or, don't use the service.

- An insurance medical release gives them rights to find out just about everything they can about you. Strike out sections that don't pertain to the coverage for which you're applying.
- Don't respond to ads for free medical information. Your name will enter more computer databases than you knew existed.

Getting a Second Opinion

Most insurance policies will pay for a second opinion. However, it's a tricky situation if you don't know the right way to do it.

- Find out your insurance company's policy regarding second opinions.
- Know the details about your condition and your physician's suggested treatment options before you seek another opinion.
- Inform your physician that you will seek a second opinion if:
  - you're unsure about your doctor's treatment choice
  - you want other options or different information
  - you want verification that what your physician has said is correct
  - your condition is life-threatening or the treatment is so major that it will irrevocably change your life
- When you get that second opinion, go outside your doctor's hospital group to do it! Do not ask your doctor for a referral. Call your local medical society.

All About Your Money

A lot has been said about money: It talks, it's the root of all evil, and it makes the world go 'round. But when money enters into a situation, people get greedy and conveniently forget to tell you the whole story. And what they're not telling is what you should know. Learn how to keep a little of that change in your own pocket instead of dropping it into theirs.

Read the Unreadable Print

The fine print is getting smaller each time you apply for a new credit card. Here are two important things you can just barely make out with a magnifying glass:

- You're liable for no more than $50 if your credit card is used fraudulently. But if you don't report the fraud within 60 days of the postmarked date on the bill, you may get stuck paying the bill to avoid taking a hit with the credit bureau.

- Not all cards charge interest the same way. Some use the average daily balance, which charges interest on your average balance for the month. Others use a two-cycle method that adds balances

FAST FACT

Shopping for interest rates? Check out several banks and then ask *your* bank to top the best offer you found.

for the current and previous month. This is more expensive, so check which method your card company uses.

Grab What You Can Get

If you're a great customer—meaning you use your card a lot and you pay on time—you can make some deals that your credit card company didn't tell you about. Use your good-customer clout to:

- have your annual fee waived
- have your interest percentage lowered (two points is a reasonable expectation)

- have a one-time late fee waived

Negotiate Your Way to Cheaper Bank Fees

What they tell you up front isn't everything there is to know. You can do better on any bank fee if you know what makes the bankers listen to you.

- Ask them to waive the loan fees. They might do it, especially if the bank is making a lot of money off your loans. They don't want you going somewhere else.

- Open another account at the same bank. The more

Rejected?

Then appeal that loan decision. Ask for a written reason—it's the law—and see where you went wrong. Then:

- Request an appeal.
- Arm yourself with new facts.
- Devise, in writing, your plan to repay the loan.
- Be persistent. If you're rejected again, go to the person above the one who rejected you.

business you do with them, the more likely they'll negotiate with you.

■ Switch to direct payment. Since they can dip right in and take it instead of waiting for you to send it, they're more likely to accommodate you.

Is Your Safe-Deposit Box Really Safe?

In many cases, yes. But valuables stored in them aren't automatically protected against loss from burglary, flood, or fire. Here are some safeguards:

■ Buy additional insurance for the contents of your box. However, be aware that most negotiable items—such as securities, bank notes, and gold— aren't covered.

■ Be able to prove your loss. Forego the secrecy and keep detailed records, appraisals, and photos.

■ Request a "safe-keeping receipt" from your bank and list all safe-deposit box contents.

■ When you open the box, ask a bank official to verify, on the receipt, the addition or removal of items.

Making a Case for Private Boxes

You don't have to rely on the bank to warehouse your valuables. Private companies offer safe-deposit boxes, too. Consider these points before making a decision:

■ Private boxes have more hours and days in which you can access them.

■ Some private boxes are insured, automatically, for $10,000.

■ Private companies usually have a higher security rating than banks.

■ Bank boxes are automatically sealed at your death. Private boxes are sealed only with a court order.

- Private boxes are harder to find because, unlike bank boxes, they aren't tagged with your bank account number.

Auditors? Oh, No!

Here's what you should know just in case the IRS comes calling:

- Ask your agent to transfer your case to another district.
- Postpone your appointment every time you can.
- Cancel it the day before it's scheduled, and odds are the next available time slot won't be for six to eight weeks.

- If you can keep your auditor away for two years, you increase your chances of having your audit canceled altogether because the IRS likes to dispatch their audits within two years.

You're Closing? I Didn't Realize...

You can outsmart the IRS if you know how to schedule your appointment the right way.

- Schedule before a three-day weekend, last appointment. No one has their mind on work then.

A Big IRS No-No

Don't go running to your congressional representative with an IRS complaint unless you're absolutely certain you're in the right. The IRS doesn't take kindly to congressional inquires, and it will go to extreme lengths to prove its innocence and let you know just how unhappy it is with you: No grace periods, no benefit of the doubt, no nothing except a cold, cold shoulder and a stab at making your tax situation most unpleasant every time the opportunity arises.

- Schedule at the end of the month. If your auditor hasn't met her case quota, she might just go easy on you so she can mark another one "closed" in her books.
- Schedule the appointment for about 10 A.M.—and eat a big breakfast. By the time the two of you are ready to discuss adjustments, it's just about lunchtime. You're well fed; she's starving. Now you can use her hunger to your advantage.

Contrary to What the IRS Says...

...you *can* take deductions without receipts. Here's how:

- Keep a diary, journal, or other written record.
- Keep photo or videotaped records.
- Get documented verification from friends or business acquaintances.

Any tangible proof of activity and expense will do, so long as it verifies the situation for which you're claiming a deduction.

Can't Make the Payment?

Don't worry. Uncle Sam won't haul you off to jail. But he can seize your bank accounts, garnish your wages, and sell your house. Here's how to stop him from trouncing all over you:

- File your tax return regardless of your ability to pay. Owing money to the IRS isn't a crime, but not filing is. By filing, you also avoid late-filing penalties.
- Pay what you can when you file.
- Contact your local IRS office to work out an installment agreement for what you owe.
- Be prepared to show proof that you can't pay.

- File all delinquent taxes before you make a payment deal. If the IRS finds out that you owe more back taxes from previous years, the deal's off and they'll demand payment in full.

Want Some Free Money?

You can claim a small reward if you do the following:

- You recognize that smarmy face on the post office mug shot board. Call your local FBI office or the national headquarters at 202-324-3000.

- You saw a cruise ship employee dump garbage overboard. Take a picture for proof and call the U.S. Coast Guard's Marine Safety and Environmental Protection division at 202-267-2200.

- You know someone who's dumping hazardous waste. Call the Environmental Protection Agency's Office of the Inspector General hotline at 888-546-8740.

- You know a tax cheater. Call the IRS at 800-829-1040.

- You can prove someone turned back the odometer on that second-hand car you just bought. Call the Auto Safety hotline at 888-327-4236.

Stretch Those Due Dates

Egads! Everything's due right now and there's not enough to go around. Fortunately, you can stretch out some payments without harming your credit rating. Typical grace periods:

- telephone company—eight days

- utilities—ten days

- banks and finance companies—ten days

So now that you know you can stretch it a little, which bills must you absolutely pay on time? Credit cards! Credit card companies submit a report to credit agencies every month, and they're likely to report you for any length of delinquency—even if it's just a few days. The least likely to nab you for falling behind is your doctor or hospital.

Checked Your Homeowners Insurance Lately?

It may cover more than you knew:

- stolen purse or wallet
- lost luggage
- property stolen in an auto break-in
- water damage inside your home's walls
- power-surge damage
- uprooted trees and bushes
- tombstone damage
- property damaged or lost when moving

Things it might not cover:

- antiques

- jewelry
- some musical instruments
- equipment for a business in your home

These items may have to be covered under a separate rider to your policy.

Just Say No!

Anything can be insured, but that doesn't mean you should run out and buy insurance for everything. Here are some popular policies you might wish to reconsider:

- Flight insurance. It's expensive, and your life insurance will pay off. Also, plane crash survivors and their families usually

FAST FACT

If you don't want to take an insurance physical, shop around. Many companies have discontinued the policy due to cost and inaccurate medical information gathered by the person conducting the tests.

Term-Life on the Cheap

If you're healthy and have no problem getting a new insurance policy—plus you renew your term-life insurance every year—switch companies every three to five years. Your premiums increase annually with your old company. A new company will start you out at the lowest first-year rate.

Best bet: Buy a fixed-rate term policy if you can find one at the right price. Many companies will lock in the rate for 10 to 20 years.

receive large cash settlements from the airline.

- Accidental death insurance. This is probably unnecessary since accidents are covered in normal life insurance policies.

- Credit insurance. This pays off your credit card debt in case of death. Term-life insurance could cost about the same for a policy that pays up to 100 times more.

Want to Check Your Credit Rating?

You don't have to pay an agency $25 or $50 to do it for you. You can do it yourself for a nominal fee. These are the three major bureaus:

Equifax
800-997-2493
www.econsumer.equifax.com

Experian
888-397-3742
www.experian.com

Trans Union
800-888-4213
www.transunion.com/
   creditreport

Credit reports from all companies cost between $8 and $10, but they're free by phone request if you're a resident of Colorado, Georgia, Maryland, Massachusetts, New Jersey, or Vermont.

Your Two Big Investments

You're paying on average $24,000 for your wheels as well as $120,000 to $220,000 for your home—depending upon the neck of the woods in which you plant yourself. That's a lot of money. So maybe it's time to learn a few things about your car and home that could surprise you.

Fuel Your Own Economy

Want to save at least 10 percent on your fuel consumption? Read on...

On the highway:

■ Observe the speed limit, which cuts down wind resistence.

■ Use overdrive, which decreases engine speed.

■ Switch on your cruise control, which helps maintain a constant speed.

In town:

■ Don't ride the brakes—or tailgate. Unnecessary braking and accelerating reduces fuel economy by 5 to 10 percent.

An Added Incentive to Slow Down

Based on the figures of $1.50 per gallon of gas in a car averaging 21 mpg at 70 mph: If you drop the speed to 65 mph, it will take you longer to get there but you'll save $5 in gas for each extra hour you drive. It will save you up to $10 if you're driving a gas-guzzling truck or an SUV.

- Don't tromp on the gas. It throws your car into the fuel-enrichment mode, which is less efficient.

Bringin' In the New Year Right

Bring it in with a new car, since New Year's Eve is one of the best days to shop for a car. New Year's Eve when it's snowing is even better. Below are car-shopping times when the advantage is in your favor:

- When there are more salespeople and cars than customers.
- Near holidays, when people are shopping for everything but cars.

- During bad weather, when no one shops.
- The end of the day, when the salesperson is tired.
- The end of the month or year. Many dealerships have sales contests for employees, and quotas usually come due at these times.

Worst time to shop: During a heavily advertised sale, because everyone else is shopping.

Trade-in Tips

The dealer will always give you the lowest trade-in price he can, so here are some steps you should take to get as much for your car as possible.

- Know the fair market price for your vehicle. Check it out in a used-car buying guide, available at libraries. Also check the Internet for used-car sites.
- Go to a used-car lot and get an offer in writing.

- Take your research with you to the dealership and show it if the offer isn't satisfactory.
- If the car is worth substantially more than the dealer's offer, demand an explanation or walk away.

Best bet: Sell that car on your own.

Hold the Finances

Don't even let them discuss financing until the last minute, because what you say can mean more cash in the dealer's pockets. Beware of these finance lines:

- "How much can you afford to pay each month?" Dealers will finance payments for as long as ten years, which is a big chunk of interest change.
- "Do you want to lease or finance that car?" If they know you're not paying cash, upping the price becomes easier since extra costs can be hidden in long-term financing.

- "Trade-in?" Trade-in offers are arbitrary, often used in lieu of discounts. Get the very best deal before you throw your trade-in into the sales pot.

Watch That Warranty, Pardner

They'll slip that extended warranty into the deal slicker than slick, when the whole dealin' match is over. But look out! That extra detail they're telling you about is shooting a load of cash right into their pockets. Here's where you could get lassoed:

- You could be buying coverage you already have. Check it out.
- The deductible may be outrageous before you can cash in on the extended coverage. Could you fix it cheaper than what you'll pay with that deductible?
- Who makes the contract good? If the work's farmed out to an independent

mechanic, who's responsible if he goes belly up?

- If you dump that buggy before the warranty expires, can you get a refund?

Turning Up the Pressure

Here are some of the oldest tricks in the car salesman's book:

- Lowballing. "It's an unbelievable deal, and if you buy today, it's yours!" When you agree, there's a reason you don't qualify. But don't worry. There are always other more expensive deals on the lot.

- Bait and switch. It's like lowballing, only the unbelievable offer is in a print ad. Naturally, someone just bought the last one at the price, but check out this other dandy over here....

- Bump up. Whatever the price, they'll try to bump it up some way: "The manager just wouldn't approve this deal, but if you're willing to..."

- The ol' turnover. They bring in the second string to "sweeten" the deal when you're not signing on their dotted line. It becomes a two-against-you negotiation at this point.

How the Dealer Learns Your Secrets

- He asks to photocopy your driver's license when you take a test drive. With that information, he'll do a quick credit report and learn the name of everyone accessing your credit history, including any other car dealers you've shopped.

- He snoops in your car during your test drive for anything that will give him more information about you.

Oily Situations

It's a slippery deal if you don't know the facts:

- You may not need an oil change every 3,000 miles. The factors dictating your need for a change are variable: number of cylinders, miles driven per year, and the kind of driving you do. An inexpensive oil analysis will tell you if your oil-changing frequency is okay.

- Synthetic oils, available in most auto supply stores, cost more, but you'll get a longer engine life and better gas mileage.

- Oil sold in quarts is a better quality than what you get in bulk at an oil change facility. When your brand is on sale, stock up.

FAST FACT

If the Quicky Lube guy says you need a new air filter, you probably do. But buy it somewhere else at a much lower cost.

Take it when you get an oil change, and ask for a discount since you didn't use their oil.

- Don't mix oil brands. It causes the oil's protective components to break down.

Movin' On Up

About to undertake some home improvements? Here are some suggestions that will increase the value and sales appeal of your home:

- anything that's energy-saving
- anything labeled as European design
- wood accents, such as counter trims and beams
- light colors and light woods
- an open kitchen
- skylights
- customized closets
- fireplaces: floor-to-ceiling stonework, mantel, and raised hearth

- high-tech lighting and dimmer switches

  extra bathroom (can bring a 130-percent recovery when you sell your house)

  richly carved wooden doors

- storm windows

Tax-Savers

The following improvements could qualify for a tax break, but check with your tax advisor for up-to-date changes in the law before you do anything.

  room additions, including porches and closets

  built-ins: cabinets, shelving, flooring

- electrical wiring

- equipment: garbage disposals, fire alarms, major appliances

- new or additional plumbing

- air conditioning, heating systems, attic fans, humidifiers, dehumidifiers

- insulation, solar heating, other energy-conservation devices

- awnings, shutters, storm doors, storm windows

- replacement roofing, gutters

- floodlights, lampposts, in-ground sprinklers

- blacktopping or other improvements to driveways

- swimming pools, tennis courts

- fences, walls, trellises, garages, carports

- shrubbery, trees

House-Selling Secrets

A homey house is always a best-seller. Here are some

house-cozying touches a prospective buyer will love:

- The smell of freshly baked bread. Stick some store-bought rolls in the oven on a very low temperature. Or sprinkle a drop or two of vanilla on a cold lightbulb, then turn on the lamp to heat it up.

- Brightly colored flowers near the outside entryway. Red geraniums in clay pots is a great choice. So is anything bright yellow. Stay away from purples, whites, and pastels, though.

- Bright, shiny doorknobs and cabinet hardware. Buy new ones if you have to.

- Family photos, old and new, especially a super-oldie of Grandma and Grandpa.

Your Broker *Will* Lower the Fee

She'll often accept a smaller commission (such as 5 percent instead of 6), especially when the market is good or when your house is an easy seller. Why? Because it won't take as much time and effort to make the deal, which is a broker's dream.

She will also accept a lower commission when the market is in a bad slump or prices are dropping. Reason: A smaller commission is better than nothing. Moreover, she'll likely accept the 5 percent if you ask her to be your agent when you buy another house, because she'll make big bucks on that deal, too.

Need Some Home Equity Bucks?

If you're over 62 and have paid off or are close to paying off your mortgage, Uncle Sam may have the best deal in town. It's called a reverse mortgage, and here's how it works:

- You receive a line of credit either as a monthly payment or a lump sum.

 INSIDE INFO

A Realtor's Big Secret

A Comparative Market Analysis (CMA) tells you ...
property values and what the houses in your neighborhood
are selling for. If you're listing your house without using a
realtor, you could be at a big disadvantage, especially if
you're asking $150,000 and nothing in your area has sold
for a penny more than $125,000. Realtors guard their
CMA, and you probably won't get a peek, even if you ask.
But their big secret is just a phone call away for you. Call
your tax assessor's office. They'll have the CMA you need.

- As long as you stay in the house, you don't have to pay it back. Payment is made when you or your survivors sell the house.

- The U.S. Department of Housing and Urban Development (HUD) collects 2 percent of the home value up front, plus ½ percent on the loan each year from insurance premiums paid by the lender. These premiums are charged to your principal balance and will cover any shortfall in sales proceeds.

- Money left over at the time of sale goes to the homeowner or survivors.

For more information, call HUD at 888-466-3487 or visit the Web site at www.hud.gov.

Getaway Guidelines

No matter if you're leaving on a jet plane or setting sail for the Caribbean, you need to be well informed to ensure a dreamy trip. Take a few minutes away from those maps and brochures and learn some lesser-known facts that will enhance

Tipping Tips

You don't have to do it if the service is poor, but a little change slipped into the right palm could earn you a friend who will make your vacation experience much more pleasant. Below are what's considered appropriate tips:

- Taxi/limo driver: $2 to $3—and more if he helps with luggage.

- Porter: $1 per bag—and more if your luggage is particularly heavy.

- Bellman: $1 per bag when he shows you to your room—and another $1 per when he helps you check out.

- Doorman: $1 for hailing a cab. Tip $1 for any extras he does, such as protecting you with an umbrella.

- Concierge: $2 to $10 for services such as making reservations or arranging sightseeing tours. Want to get the best service? Tip $10 to $20 up front. Also, if you don't have tickets to someplace you're dying to go, ask the concierge. He's on the in with the best places and can get you

FAST FACT

To avoid over-tipping when traveling, always carry an ample supply of small bills and change.

When You End Up in Newark but Your Bags Go to Maui...

- Report lost luggage immediately.
- Provide a complete list of contents.
- Ask for fair compensation, on the spot, to buy enough clothing and toiletries to tide you over until your bags are found. Airlines rarely volunteer the money, but many will provide it if you ask.

there even without advance reservations.

- Hotel maid: $1 per night, left in an envelope marked "maid."
- Parking attendant: $1 to $2 when car is delivered.
- Waiters: 15 to 20 percent of your *pre-tax* check.

Secrets of the Innkeeper

His toll-free number is the *last* number you want to call if you're trying to make a reservation with a large hotel chain. Toll-free operators are not flexible in price adjustments and will offer only the standard "rack rate." But reservation clerks in the actual hotel are ready and able to make a deal. Here's how to get one:

- Ask "What's your best rate?" or "Can you do better?"
- If you've stayed there before, ask them to match your previous rate.
- Are you an association or military member? Senior citizen? Ask what groups get discounts.
- Have a business card? Maybe you'll qualify for a corporate rate.

Baggage Basics

Less is best. It means a shorter wait in the claims

line, less need for porters, and an easier trip through customs. These are baggage facts you should know:

- If it's not in good shape, airlines can refuse to carry it.
- Carry-on baggage restrictions can apply to briefcases. So that you don't get caught, limit your carry-ons to only one other piece when you're toting a briefcase.
- Two carry-ons is a general rule, but it could be changed at the discretion of the flight attendant. Thus, pack your "absolutely must haves" in your smallest bag.

You're Going Where?

Maybe Afghanistan is off the beaten tourist path, but if that's your dream vacation spot, you'd better check the travel warnings issued by the State Department. For any country in question, search www.travel.state.gov for the latest information about:

- coups
- bomb threats
- terrorist violence
- chemical and biological warfare

While you're at it, contact the Centers for Disease Control to learn about epidemics and outbreaks in your chosen destination. Call 877-FYI-TRIP or visit the Web site at www.cdc.gov.

American Passports Mean Big $$$

So when you travel abroad:

- Make two passport copies. Leave one at home and carry the other with you, apart from your original passport.
- Carry proof of citizenship, identification, and two extra passport photos in case you have to apply for another on your trip.
- Know where to find the nearest U.S. Embassy or Consulate in every destination along your journey,

and contact them immediately if your passport is stolen.

Thieves know just how to spot a tourist with a ripe-for-the-picking passport, so when you're traveling, you need to know how to keep yours safe. Don't keep it in:

- over-the-shoulder bags
- backpacks and fanny packs
- your car

Safest place: In a zippered belt under your clothes—or in the hotel safe.

This 'n' That

Here's some great advice for any trip you take:

- For added safety, use your own rubber doorstopper in a hotel.
- Use disposable cameras.
- Attach small bells to the outside of your luggage to let you know if someone's trying to steal it. Luggage alarms can be purchased from luggage dealers, too.

- For personal safety, don't put your address on your luggage. Instead, use a business address or the address of a contact other than a personal one, such as a church or lodge.
- Don't look wealthy. Dress in plain clothes and buy a cheap watch just for the trip.

Secrets of Cleaner Travel

You just never know how many hundreds of people have been there before you. To make your travel a little more sanitary:

- Check out the cleanliness of your cruise ship by contacting the Centers For Disease Control's vessel sanitation program at www.cdc.gov/nceh/vsp/vsp.htm.
- Take along your own travel pillow on the plane. Airplanes make several stops a day, but pillows get

changed only once or twice.

- Although they have maids, hotel rooms aren't clean. Carry a can of disinfectant and give everything a good dousing, including the phone.

- The guy who used the pay phone right before you spent ten minutes coughing and sneezing all over it. Pull out the hand wipes or a can of disinfectant.

How Many Extra Charges Can They Tack On to One Car Rental?

A whole bunch. Here are just a few:

- Drop-off charge: It's added when you drop off the car in a city other than that in which it was rented.

- Collision Damage Waiver or Loss Damage Waiver: Releases you from financial responsibility if you wreck the car.

- Personal Accident Insurance: Provides accidental death and medical coverage.

- Personal Effects Coverage: Covers loss or theft of personal belongings.

- Additional Liability Insurance: Protects you from a third-party lawsuit.

FAST FACT

Taxes on international car rentals can be as high as 30 percent—in addition to the rate quoted. Better check them out before you sign on the dotted line.

Here's how to beat some of the extra costs:

- Your own car insurance policy may cover everything you need. Read it before you rent.

- Many credit card companies kick in necessary insurances if you use their card for the rental.

- Call several rental car companies.

Givin' It the Gas

Filling up is not necessarily a requirement when you return your rental. Here are your options:

1. Bring the car back full.

2. Bring it back empty and let the rental company fill it up. They charge by the gallon and usually tack on a huge per-gallon service fee.

3. Prepurchase a tank-full, at the time of rental, for a flat fee. You don't have to refuel the car when you return it.

Best bet: Fill it up yourself—from the cheapest gas station you can find. When the rental agency gets involved in your fill-up, it's gonna cost you an arm and a leg.

■ Ask for a better deal. Unhappy customers can usually finagle an upgrade.

Hey, Honey, Maybe You Should Ask...

Unless you have built-in radar, you're going to get lost from time to time if you take many car trips. Here are a few tips that might help if you're one of those who'd rather rip out your teeth with pliers than stop and ask for directions:

■ Major highways that are even-numbered and have one or two digits run east and west.

■ Major highways that are odd-numbered and have one or two digits run north and south.

■ Three digits starting with an even number circle a city.

■ Three digits starting with an odd number run to or from the city center.

Holiday Travel Tips

Getting from here to there can be difficult, since everybody else is trying to do it, too. Here are the top five holidays for travel:

1. Christmas/New Year period
2. Thanksgiving weekend
3. Easter week
4. Washington's Birthday weekend
5. Labor Day weekend

If you find yourself on the road during these peak times, follow these tips to make your holiday travel happier:

- Depart or drive during off-peak hours to avoid traffic.
- When flying, don't wrap carry-on gifts. They may be unwrapped at the security gate.

Thinking About Escaping the Holiday Rush?

European countries celebrate the following:

- Christmas, New Year's Day, and Boxing Day (December 26)
- New Year's Day on January 2 in Bulgaria, Czechoslovakia, Hungary, Turkey, and Yugoslavia
- Good Friday and Easter (Easter is a Monday holiday in most countries)
- May Day
- national holidays (check with the tourist board of the country in which you plan to travel)

Plan your trip accordingly, and make sure you don't end up in a cash crunch on a foreign holiday.

For a cruise or other booked tour, consider purchasing cancellation insurance in case your holiday plans change.

Prepay before you go so there'll be room at the inn when you get there.

Bad, Bad Trip

That three-hour tour your travel agent planned for you turned out to be a dud, but no one's going to just hand you back your money. It's up to you to fight for it. So prepare yourself in advance:

Keep brochures and other printed materials given to you by the travel agent.

Keep evidence of problems and unkept promises from the agency, such as receipts and photos.

Take this to your travel agent and ask for a refund. Put your request in writing, too.

If you fail to get results, and your travel agent is a member of the American Society of Travel Agents (ASTA), contact them at:

American Society of Travel Agents (ASTA) Consumer Affairs
1101 King Street
Alexandria, VA 22314

Follow these criteria:

1. The firm against which you are complaining must have had adequate time to respond to you before you file a complaint with ASTA.

2. The case cannot have been brought into previous litigation.

3. Your problem occurred within the past six months.

4. Your complaint is in writing with supporting documents.

10 Last, But Not Least . . .

It is so difficult to keep up in our complex, fast-paced society that you need every edge you can get. To round out this book, here are a few more tidbits that can make a difference in your life, no matter if you're looking for a better way to plan a move or simply get your car washed.

Get Movin'!

Moving is one of the most stressful events in people's lives. Here are a few things you should add to your to-do list:

- Change your address with both the post office and the IRS.

- Send mailers, available from the post office, with your new address to everyone who's important. Check your magazines for their change-of-address policy.

- Save your moving receipts, since expenses could be deductible.

- Check with your insurance agent to see how your property is covered in transit.

Got the picture? There are 1,001 things to do. To learn everything you need to know about moving, including how to move your gorilla, visit the MoversNet Web site at www.usps.gov/moversnet.

Best of Times

Here are a few times that will make your life easier:

- Video rental: Friday morning, before the weekend crowd stocks up on the favorites. Or Tuesday, the day when most of the new ones arrive.

- Library: Friday night, when the students are partying instead of studying.

- Hospital stay: Any month other than June or July, when the fresh-out-of-school doctors arrive. And any time other than holiday weeks, when hospitals are typically short-staffed.

- Carwash: Monday or Tuesday, when the weekend rush is over and the next weekend rush hasn't begun.

- Business phone calls: First and last hours of the business day, because most people are at their desks then.

- Grocery shopping: Early Friday morning, when the store's shelves are fully stocked for the weekend onslaught.

Check Your Check

No, it probably won't get away from you, but if it does, here's how to make sure the sticky-finger who picks it up and tries to cash it can't:

- Before you go to the bank, write "for deposit only" on it. Make sure the words are bold, dark, and legible so they'll be difficult to tamper with.

- Sign your name below the words.

- Write your account number below your signature. Again, make it bold, dark, and legible.

This way, if that check does manage to escape, it can be deposited *only* into your account.

You Know That Wool Sweater That Used to Fit?

You don't have to run out and buy another one. Here's how to unshrink that wool:

1. Mix two tablespoons of baby shampoo, or a detergent specifically for wool, with one gallon of lukewarm water.

2. Soak your diminutive wool garment for ten minutes.

3. Remove from the suds, but do not rinse or wring.

4. Stretch it out on a towel, and blot it with another towel.

5. Reshape it into something that fits.

6. Leave it there to dry. Keep it away from direct sunlight and heat.

Let's Play Find the Fat!

On the menu, that is. Those restaurant people have many sneaky ways to hide the fat. While it tastes wonderful cooked up in almost any dish, it's usually not a healthy choice. However, you can win this little hide-and-seek game if you know the terms.

- ■ "Au frommage" or "au gratin" mean there's some cheese hiding in it someplace.

- ■ "À la mode" is served with ice cream.

- ■ "Bisque" means it's a cream-based soup.

- ■ "Au lait" is with milk.

- ■ "Escalloped," "scalloped," and "hollandaise" all come in cream sauce.

- ■ "Sauté" means it's cooked in fat.

The Food of the Gods

We crave chocolate. We worship it. And they keep telling us it's bad for us. Well, it's not as bad as you might think.

- ■ It doesn't cause acne. Hormones do that.

- ■ It's not addictive—just a habit.

- ■ It's not overloaded with caffeine: Eight ounces of chocolate milk has five milligrams of caffeine, whereas five ounces of regular coffee has 115.

- ■ Its saturated fat content, which comes from stearic

Snack Facts

From the American Dietetic Association:

- Seventy-five percent of all men and women snack at least once a day.
- Snacks take the edge off hunger and help keep you from overeating.
- Snacks are responsible for one-third of a preschooler's energy.
- TV watching increases snacking, particularly on high-fat, high-calorie foods.

acid, isn't harmful to your blood vessels. It doesn't raise your cholesterol, either. *However,* that smooth, rich taste of milk chocolate comes from butter fat, which can clog your arteries. Dark chocolate is the best choice.

Morning Goodness

It gets you going. It opens your eyes. It gives you a reason for living. But in some cases, coffee comes with its risks.

- People with high blood pressure: It can raise it.

- Women trying to conceive: It can reduce the likelihood by up to 50 percent.
- Men who are trying to father: It can increase the number of abnormal sperm.
- Those with digestive disorders: It can irritate the stomach lining.
- Headache sufferers: It causes alternate constriction and dilation of blood vessels, which leads to headaches.

And...

- Women who drink four or more cups a day are twice

as likely to develop breast cysts.

- It's been linked to ovarian cancer and premenstrual syndrome.

A Big Headache

That's what you'll get if the headrests in your car aren't adjusted properly and you get into an accident. Here's the right way:

- Adjust your head restraint as close to the top of your head as possible—and no less than 3½ inches below it.

- It must touch the back of your head but not your neck.

- Position your seat as close to vertical as possible.

Check the headrests before you buy a car. If they don't meet the safety criteria, consider that two-thirds of all people injured in car accidents have neck injuries—then reconsider the car you want to buy.

Sick Without the Sun

We know too much sun can cause deadly skin cancer, but too little has its own set of health problems. They include:

- Weakened bones. The sun produces vitamin D, which helps the body absorb calcium. Calcium strengthens bones, and without vitamin D, the calcium isn't getting to them.

- Arthritis. A lack of sun doesn't cause it, but the sun's vitamin D does slow the progression.

- Cancer. Studies indicate that Vitamin D may inhibit the development of several kinds: breast, colon, and prostate.

Best solution: Go for a short walk in the sun every day. Also, drink milk and eat plenty of fish to get your necessary vitamin D.

Ahhh. . .So Romantic

But oh, so deadly. Candles cause nearly 9,000 major fires each year, killing about 100 people and injuring about 1,000.

Half of all home candle fires start in the bedroom.

December is by far the worst month for candle fires.

Here are some candle tips:

Snuff them when you leave the room or go to sleep.

Keep them away from clothing, books, paper, curtains, bedding, and Christmas trees.

Secure them in a steady holder that catches wax.

Keep them out of the paths of kids and pets.

Don't carry a lit candle.

Keep them away from emergency equipment, such as a kerosene heater or a lantern.

How to Survive a Carjacking

The rule is: Do anything it takes to save your life! Here are some tips to make that happen:

■ Avoid driving in areas you know to be dangerous.

■ When driving in an unfamiliar area, take someone else along.

■ Roll up your windows and lock the doors.

■ Check your mirrors regularly.

■ Leave room to maneuver out of an area when you come to a stop.

■ If bumped from behind, and you think it was on purpose, don't get out. Ask him to follow you to a well-lighted, heavily populated area or to the nearest police station.

■ Park in well-lighted areas in plain view of others.

■ Approach your car with keys in hand. Check

underneath the car before you get there, then check the front and rear seats before you get in.

■ If you are confronted by a carjacker, give up the keys and car (remember, it's insured). Don't resist.

Puffer Facts

Of course, you already know that smoking is dangerous. But here's the lowdown on those "low tars and nicotines" just in case you think they're safer:

■ The advertised tar and nicotine levels are determined by puffing robots, not humans.

■ The numbers don't represent actual amounts of tar and nicotine inhaled because robots don't inhale the way people do, and no two people inhale alike.

■ Many low-tar cigarettes have vents that allow air to dilute the smoke, but those vents can close up without the smoker knowing it.

■ Low-nicotine smokers inhale deeper and more frequently than smokers who use regular cigarettes, which means they're getting more anyway.

Bottom line: No matter how it's packaged, there's no such thing as a safe smoke.

Sleeping With a Buzz Saw?

That loud, shake-the-rafters snoring could mean sleep apnea, a condition where someone stops breathing while they sleep. It's caused by a blockage in the airway, and while millions are afflicted, most don't know it.

Here's who are most susceptible:

■ men
■ those overweight
■ those over age 40

And here's what can happen if it's not treated:

Muffle That Snore

Elevate the head of your bed with a brick under each leg.

Use one pillow per customer. Toss the extras.

Skip the depressants before bedtime: booze, tranquilizers, sleeping pills, antihistamines.

Drop some pounds. Seventy-five percent of all heavy snorers are overweight.

Wear a cervical collar. It keeps your chin up and your airway unobstructed.

Use one of those adhesive nasal strips to open your nasal valves.

high blood pressure

heart disease

memory problems

weight gain

headaches

impotence

If you're tired and sleepy all the time, or the person with whom you sleep complains that your snoring can be heard three blocks away, it could mean you're experiencing sleep apnea. Get help! For more information, visit the American Sleep Apnea Association Web site at www.sleepapnea.org, or call 202-293-3560.

Are You a Front-Load or a Top?

It makes a difference in the energy you use and the money you save. Front-load washers are a little more costly to buy, but they make up for the extra bucks in these savings:

■ They use less water— one-third to one-half the amount of water as top-load washers.

- They require less gas or electricity.
- They spin faster, wring the clothes better, and reduce dryer time and cost.

If you're considering a front-loader, contact your utility company first. Many will give you an incentive to make the purchase.

To get the best energy value from any washer:

- Load the washer to its capacity.
- Use cold-water rinses.
- Set your water heater thermostat to no higher than 120 degrees.

Feel Secure?

Once every couple years, check your Social Security contributions against the amount with which you're being credited. There could be mistakes.

- Visit the Web site at www.ssa.gov and fill out the online form. You'll receive an Earnings and Benefit Estimate Statement in two to four weeks.
- Call 800-772-1213 and ask for Form SSA-7004. After you've sent it in, your statement will arrive in four to six weeks.
- If your contributions (you can get this information from your employer) don't match your record, call 800-772-1213 to learn how to resolve the problem. You have three years, three months, and 15 days after the year in which the wages were paid to correct the error.

Slash Your Funeral Costs

It's a stressful time, and the funeral directors know it. That's why they don't tell you how to make the best choices. Normally, they just offer a package deal. But the law requires them to provide you with a list breaking down services and costs so that you can make informed choices. Here are ways to save some money:

- The mortuary as a viewing or funeral-service facility: A church will work just as well, without the heavy cost.

- Embalming: This is not required by law in most cases. Refrigeration is cheaper and will do just as well.

- Cremation: This is about one-tenth the cost of burial.

- Makeup: This may be good for an open casket, but it's not necessary if it's closed.

- Obituary notices: Consider writing the obituary to save the cost of someone else doing it.

- Clergy and organist: You can provide your own, but neither are necessary for a funeral service. It depends on your personal beliefs and desires.

All About Caskets

We've gone from a simple pine box to something that, in many cases, costs more than your car. But there are alternatives here, too:

- Caskets online. Even with overnight shipping costs, you can save hundreds of dollars. And the varieties —including denim for cowboys and do-it-yourself kits for the handyman—will amaze you. Search the word *caskets* for a service you didn't know existed.

- Rent-a-casket. Most mortuaries rent caskets to those who choose cremation. However, even if you're not considering cremation, you can ask for a rental to use for the viewing. For the actual burial, you could buy something simple and cheap, like an actual cremation casket, which is made of cardboard or plywood.

For more information on funeral details, visit the Funeral and Memorial Society of America Web site at www.funerals.org/famsa.

Entertainment on the Cheap

Finding quality entertainment for an evening doesn't have to cost a day's pay. Here are some ways to have a great time without a great cost:

■ Work for it. You know those ushers you see at sporting events? They actually get paid to be there—and the game is free.

■ Volunteer for it. Many cultural activities rely on volunteer ushers.

■ Check out the universities. They sponsor lectures, movies, recitals, and live performances at a fraction of the cost of the professional equivalent. Check out what the high schools have to offer, too.

■ Get your movie from the library instead of the video rental stores. It's usually free.

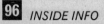